Our Flag

I KNOW AMERICA

Eleanor Ayer

THE MILLBROOK PRESS
Brookfield, Connecticut

Published by The Millbrook Press
2 Old New Milford Road
Brookfield, CT 06804
© 1992 Blackbirch Graphics, Inc.
First Edition

Created and produced in association with Blackbirch Graphics.
Series Editor: Bruce S. Glassman

Library of Congress Cataloging-in-Publication Data
Ayer, Eleanor H.
    Our flag / Eleanor H. Ayer.
    Includes bibliographical references and index.
    Summary: Examines the history, usage, and etiquette of the American flag.
    ISBN 1-56294-107-0
    1. Flags—United Sates—History. Juvenile literature. [1. Flags—United
States—History.] I. Title. II. Series.
JC346.Z3A94   1992
929.9'2'0973—dc20   91-38892
                                                                         CIP
                                                                          AC

Acknowledgments and Photo Credits
Cover: ©Chuck Peterson; Back cover photo: Bill Swersey/Gamma-Liaison;
p. 4: ©Arnold J. Kaplan/The Picture Cube; pp. 7, 14, 15, 16, 18, 20, 21: The
Library of Congress Collection; p. 9: ©Bob Daemmrich/The Image Works;
pp. 10, 25: Bettmann; p. 23: Culver Pictures, Inc.; p. 28: North Wind Picture
Archives; p. 34: ©William Clark/Department of the Interior; p. 37: © J. Isaac/
The United Nations; p. 40: Wide World Photos; p. 42: ©Doug Mills/Wide
World Photos, Inc.; p. 45: NASA.

Photo Research by **Inge King.**

CONTENTS

INTRODUCTION

"The Star-Spangled Banner" . . . "The Stars and Stripes" . . . "Old Glory" . . . Are there colors that come into your mind when you see those words? Do you hear music in your head? These are a few of the nicknames for the flag that you see flying all across our nation every day.

Seeing Old Glory waving from a tall pole, or "mast," gives most Americans a feeling of pride. For some it causes goosebumps and brings tears to their eyes. We are often proud of what Americans before us have done. We are proud of the values for which America stands. Because we are proud of our country, we are also proud of our flag.

Whether our flag flies on the moon or hangs on a bedroom wall, it is a symbol of what makes America great. One of our country's many patriotic songs, "It's My Flag, Too," reminds us that Old Glory is a symbol of truth and right:

The fairest flag beneath the sun,
The flag that glorious freedom won,
That tells of deeds of valor done,
With pride we view;
Its shining folds of red and white,
Stream out like beams of morning light:
And e'er stands firm for truth and right.
It's my flag too.

The American flag stands for freedom. Americans are free to speak and write their ideas without fear of punishment, as long as they do not hurt or deny the rights of others. Americans are free to make statements against the government if they disagree with it. In the United States, people are free to travel, to work at jobs of their choice, to worship as they wish, and to live where they are able. These are some freedoms that are not possible in many countries. Most Americans take pride in these freedoms and in the flag that stands for them.

The American flag also stands for the bravery of many people. Throughout our country's history, millions of Americans have died or put their lives in danger to defend our flag. During the 1860s, the American Civil

War was fought over slavery and other questions. Northern soldiers fought against those from the Southern states. When General Stonewall Jackson's Southern troops marched into the northern town of Frederick, Maryland, they saw an American flag flying from the window of a house. Legend says that in that house lived a woman named Barbara Frietchie. When General Jackson ordered his troop to fire on her flag, she is said to have stuck her head out the window and dared Jackson to shoot. The American poet John Greenleaf Whittier made Barbara's words famous in his poem, "Barbara Frietchie": "'Shoot, if you must, this old gray head, But spare your country's flag,' she said."

The American flag stands for accomplishment and success. Through the years, American explorers, scientists, writers, entertainers, teachers, business people, and other leaders have been among the best

Barbara Frietchie became famous in the 1860s when she courageously defended Old Glory. She dared Southern troops to shoot her instead of the flag.

in the world. They have made us proud to be Americans and proud of the flag that stands for America. In the 1988 Olympics, American sprinter Florence Griffith Joyner ran a victory lap after winning her medal. In her hand, flying from an aluminum pole, she proudly carried the Stars and Stripes.

Old Glory in Our Culture

Many Americans who are proud of their flag have remembered Old Glory in songs, poems, paintings, postage stamps, and other patriotic settings. One of the most famous pictures of the flag shows a scene from the Revolutionary War. Americans were fighting this war to become free from unfair British rule. On Christmas night, 1776, General George Washington and some American troops set out across the ice-filled Delaware River in small boats. They planned to make a surprise attack on enemy soldiers. A hundred years later, a painting was made of this famous crossing. Rising proudly from the center of Washington's boat is the Stars and Stripes.

There is only one problem with the painting. The battle happened six months before that banner was approved as America's first flag!

Washington Crossing the Delaware was even the subject of a postage stamp. In fact, of all the designs the Postal Service has used on stamps, the flag is the most popular. The American flag has been the subject of more than thirty stamps, and has been part of the picture in another forty. No matter what the current rate for a first-class letter, there is usually a flag stamp for that amount.

Many singers and performers have used Old Glory in their acts. A flag cloth was wrapped around the actor Sylvester Stallone in the *Rocky* movies, a popular series of films about a boxer. In *Rocky IV*, when he beats a Russian boxer, Rocky's shorts are even designed like an American flag. Rocky wasn't the first entertainer to wear the flag. Back in the 1910s the Dolly Sisters, a song and dance team, also wrapped themselves in Old Glory.

Our flag offers us a way to express our feelings about our country. When people are proud of the United States, they fly the flag from their porches or hang it in windows. At times of national sorrow, flags fly at half-mast—only halfway up the flag pole—as a symbol of Americans' grief. People who are angry with the country have burned the flag to show that they disagree with or do not support the United States. However we feel about our country, the flag helps us show those feelings, because the Stars and Stripes is a symbol of America.

How We Act Around the Flag

We show our pride in the flag by acting in a respectful way around it. When we say the Pledge of Allegiance, we stand and put our right hands over our hearts. Men take off their hats. Military people salute. When "The Star-Spangled Banner" is played, we stand and face the flag, just as we do when we recite the Pledge.

We show respect for the flag by putting our hands over our hearts when we say the Pledge of Allegiance.

THE
EARLIEST FLAGS

For more than one hundred years, the flags of other countries flew over what is now America. At that time there was no Stars and Stripes. There was no United States. Explorers coming to the New World brought with them the flags of their own countries.

One of the first Englishmen to explore America was John Cabot, in 1497. Cabot carried the flag of England, which was then the Cross of Saint George. This flag showed a large red cross on a *field*, or background, of white. By 1607, when English settlers arrived at Jamestown in the colony of Virginia, a white X-shaped cross had been added to their flag. This cross of Saint Andrew was for Scotland, whose king

Opposite:
John Cabot carried the flag of England when he first landed in America.

11

had become king of England. The red and white crosses, woven on a field of blue, made up Great Britain's Union Flag. From the mid-1600s until the Revolutionary War, the American colonies flew this British flag because they were ruled by England. A third cross—a red *X* broken in the center—was later added for Ireland when it, too, was brought into the United Kingdom. This design, called the Union Jack, is the flag of the United Kingdom today. Many other flags, like those from Australia, New Zealand, and provinces in Canada have incorporated the Union Jack design into their designs as well.

FLAG TALK

There are many names for flags. A flag can be called an *ensign*. That's the word sailors often use for the flag on a ship. The ensign shows the ship's country. When a fleet, or a group of ships, is traveling together, the first ship carries the fleet's flag. This is the flagship.

Sometimes the word *jack* is used to talk about naval flags. Britain's flag is called the Union Jack. Through the years there have been many kinds of union jacks. Most have had red and white crosses on a background of blue.

A flag can be called a *standard*. A military officer or soldier who carries the flag is the standard bearer. We also use the phrase *the colors* to speak of the flag. When a man is "called to the colors," he is asked to serve his country and his flag in the military. In the navy, the colors are raised at 8:00 each morning. At sunset when the flag is taken down, we say the colors have been "struck." During war, when a country must surrender, it is ordered to "strike the colors" as a sign of defeat.

Flags of the Colonies and Towns

In 1686, colonists in New England decided they would like a flag just for their area. They borrowed their design from a British banner popular at the time, the Red Ensign. The Red Ensign used the red Cross of Saint George in a white *canton*, the upper left corner of the flag. The rest of the flag was a field of red, although some flag historians claim the field was blue. The Cross of Saint George divided the canton into four white squares. In the upper left square the proud New Englanders put a green pine tree. This was the New England flag. It flew proudly ninety years later at the Battle of Bunker Hill in Massachusetts—the first major battle of the Revolutionary War.

By the last half of the 1700s, there was much tension between England and the American colonies. The colonists did not want the English government to tax them. They wanted to pass their own laws in their own legislatures. In the city of Boston stood a large grove of elm trees. One of these marked the meeting place of the Sons of Liberty. The Sons were a group of colonists who were getting ready to fight the British. At the Liberty Tree they raised the first Liberty flag. It was a simple pattern of nine red and white stripes. A thirteen-stripe version of this flag flew on December 16, 1773, during the Boston Tea Party. On that famous date, American colonists took action. Tired of the taxes the British charged on tea and other goods, the colonists dressed up as Indians and dumped a ship-load of British tea into Boston Harbor.

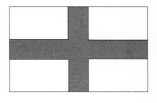

The Cross of St. George.

13

Above:
The first flag of the United American Colonies flew during the Boston Tea Party in 1773.

Below:
Colonists who organized the Boston Tea Party were protesting unfair taxes imposed by the British.

The red and white stripes of the Liberty flag were used in the first flag of the United American Colonies. This new flag had thirteen red and white stripes—one for each of the colonies. The stripes took up the whole flag; there was no canton.

Even though this flag stood for all the colonies, it was not the only flag flown throughout the land. Some of the colonies and many of the towns had their own flags. The people of Taunton, Massachusetts, used the British design in their town's flag. They placed it in the canton with a field of red around it. At the bottom, in white, was the phrase "Liberty and Union." Patriotic words like these were popular on flags for many years.

Battle Flags

As the colonies moved closer to war with England, ships were made ready for a navy. Christopher Gadsden, a government leader from South Carolina, thought the navy's flagship should have a very special flag. The design he liked had a field of yellow with a coiled rattlesnake sitting in the center. At the bottom was the phrase *Don't Tread on Me.*

The snake had long been a symbol of wisdom. During the American Revolution, it was a symbol of defiance against England. Americans were saying, "We will no longer be treated unfairly by the English government." Earlier colonial flags used the timber rattlesnake, a kind of snake that lived only in America. This was the one chosen for the Gadsden flag. Other American flags would also use the rattlesnake. In the first navy jack of 1775, the snake was stretched out to full length across a field of red and white stripes. The words *Don't Tread on Me* went with the rattler on most flags.

A different style of flag was used during the Revolution by some ships that General George Washington fitted out for use around Boston. This group was called Washington's Cruisers, and its ensign was a large pine tree on a field of white. The pine tree had been used earlier on New England flags. At the bottom of

Patriot Colonel Christopher Gadsden designed the "Don't Tread on Me" flag and presented it to the Continental Congress.

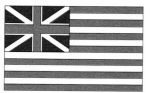

John Paul Jones is known as the first man to ever hoist the Grand Union flag (above).

the Washington's Cruisers' flag was the phrase, "An Appeal to Heaven" (or sometimes just written as "Appeal to Heaven"). The flag asked God to help the struggling colonists win their freedom from Great Britain.

It was becoming clear that Americans needed one flag that could be flown by all groups: army, navy, towns, and colonies. The new banner used the

British Union flag in the canton to show that the colonies were still a part of Britain. But the field was thirteen red and white stripes, one for each of the colonies that people hoped would soon be free from England. There were many names for the new flag: Continental Colors, Grand Union, and Great Union. It was hoisted for the first time on December 3, 1775. On that day, the continental banner flew from the *Alfred*, the flagship of America's new navy. The man who first hoisted it, John Paul Jones, would soon be famous as a navy hero.

THE MEANING OF COLORS

The red, white, and blue flag is a symbol of the United States of America. But what do those colors symbolize? There are no sure answers to that question. Many writers have suggested reasons why red, white, and blue were chosen for our flag. Some say red stands for the blood that so many Americans have shed fighting for this country. To some, white is a symbol of loyalty—Americans' promise to be true and faithful to the United States flag. Blue, some people say, is for unity—fifty states and millions of people who are bound together as one nation.

The government has never said why red, white, and blue were chosen. The only mention of colors by lawmakers is in a report to the Continental Congress from its secretary, Charles Thomson. While talking about the Seal of the United States, Thomson said that parts of it would be red, white, and blue, like the flag. "White signifies purity and innocence, Red, hardiness and valour, and Blue . . . vigilance, perseverance and justice."

FLAGS OF A GROWING NATION

On July 2, 1776, Americans boldly declared their independence. They declared themselves to be free from English rule. Two days later, government leaders signed the Declaration of Independence. It said that the thirteen colonies were now "free and independent states." One of the men who signed the Declaration of Independence was Francis Hopkinson. He also helped design the new country's first flag. The design used the red and white stripes from earlier flags, but added something never before used: stars.

   Some flag historians say that Hopkinson had very little or no part in designing the first American flag. No one is sure just how much of the design was

Opposite:
General George Washington watches as the first Stars and Stripes is raised in 1777.

19

THE STORY OF A SEAMSTRESS

For many years Americans thought a woman had made the first flag. She was said to be Elizabeth (Betsy) Ross, a seamstress from Philadelphia. The story started when Mrs. Ross's grandson, William Canby, made a speech to the Pennsylvania Historical Society. He said his grandmother had met with General Washington to make plans for the new flag. Betsy Ross was, indeed, a flagmaker. But historians can find no proof that she made the first American flag.

On display at the Chicago World's Fair in 1893 was a picture called *Birth of Our Nation's Flag.* It showed Betsy Ross and her helpers working on the Stars and Stripes. The picture became very popular. Across America people gave ten cents apiece to help turn Betsy Ross's Philadelphia home into a museum. Each person who gave a dime to the museum got a copy of the picture. The story of Betsy Ross was told in schoolbooks. In 1952, the post office printed Betsy's picture on a stamp. Even though most historians say the story is not true, Betsy Ross has become an American legend.

Betsy Ross and her helpers show the flag to George Washington.

his. But one idea, at least, came from a book in Hopkinson's library. In the book was a bookplate on which the owner could write his name. The picture on the bookplate was Hopkinson's family seal, or coat of arms. In the center of the seal were three six-pointed stars. From this bookplate, the idea for the stars on Old Glory was born.

The Stars and Stripes Becomes Official

The U.S. Congress made the Stars and Stripes America's official flag on June 14, 1777. Said the lawmakers: "The flag of the United States [will] be thirteen stripes, alternate red and white [and] . . . the union [canton] be thirteen stars, white in a blue field, representing a new constellation." The new country of America was like a new constellation, or group of stars in the sky.

Although June 14 became the birthday of Old Glory in 1777, there were no big birthday parties for many years. Some towns held their own celebrations, but there were no special events nationwide. In 1916, President Woodrow Wilson proclaimed June 14 Flag Day. Each state, he said, could celebrate Flag Day as it wished. Some states held celebrations, but still June 14 was not a holiday nationwide. At last, on August 3, 1949, President Harry Truman signed an official act of Congress making June 14 National Flag Day. All Americans across the country would now celebrate the flag's birthday together.

Francis Hopkinson (above) is thought to be one of the original designers of the Stars and Stripes.

The first Stars and Stripes had thirteen stars and thirteen stripes to represent the thirteen colonies.

21

In its 1777 proclamation, Congress did not say just how the thirteen stars should be placed on the new flag. At first there were five rows in the canton, some with three stars and some with two. Many paintings of the flag showed the stars in a circle. That summer an important battle of the Revolutionary War was fought at Bennington, Vermont. The Stars and Stripes is thought to have been carried in that battle. But the design of that flag was a little different. The top and bottom stripes were white instead of red. The canton had two stars in the top corners. The other eleven were grouped in an arch below. Inside the arch was the date of independence: 76.

For the next few years, as our country grew, a new stripe was added to the flag every time a new state joined the union. In the beginning there were thirteen stars and thirteen stripes for the thirteen states. When Vermont and Kentucky became states in 1791 and 1792, two more stars and two more stripes were added. America then had a fifteen-stripe flag. This flag flew while our first four presidents were in office.

The Battle at Fort McHenry

The fifteen-stripe flag was flying at Fort McHenry, Maryland, on the night of September 13, 1814. That night the fort was attacked by the British. They were fighting the Americans in the War of 1812. On the deck of a ship in Chesapeake Bay stood a young

American lawyer named Francis Scott Key. All through the night, Key watched the fighting and "the bombs bursting in air." But he couldn't tell who was winning the battle.

The next morning, "by the dawn's early light," Francis Scott Key saw something that showed him the Americans had won. What he saw was the fifteen-stripe American flag still flying at Fort McHenry. So proud and happy was Key that he wrote a poem about the flag, "The Star-Spangled Banner." That poem later became our national anthem. The same flag that waved "o're the land of the free and the home of the brave" at Fort McHenry now hangs at the Smithsonian Institution's National Museum of American History in Washington, D.C. The Smithsonian is fondly called "America's attic," for many important items from America's past are stored and displayed there.

By 1817, five more states had joined the Union. The flag now needed twenty stripes. But space was getting tight on Old Glory. A group of congressmen met to talk about the problem. They decided that the number of stripes should go back to thirteen—one for each of the thirteen original colonies. Only new stars would be added. Each year that new states joined the Union, the flag would be changed on July 4 to add new stars. This rule was part of the Flag Act of 1818. Never again would the American flag have more than thirteen stripes.

Most Americans didn't fly the flag often in the early 1800s. But in times of war, people became more

Francis Scott Key watched the battle at Fort McHenry from a British ship in the Chesapeake Bay, near Baltimore.

patriotic. This was especially true during the Mexican War of 1846. Mexico and the United States began fighting after the United States made Texas a state and took over much of the other land along the Mexican-American border. In the Mexican War, for the first time, American troops carried the Stars and Stripes with them into battle.

Suddenly people wanted flags to fly in support of their troops. But the country was growing so fast that many Americans had a hard time finding a flag with the right number of stars. When the Mexican War ended in 1848, America had a thirty-star flag. By 1851 the flag had thirty-one stars. In 1858, another was added. By 1859, Old Glory was up to thirty-three stars. Two years later, the thirty-fourth star was added for Kansas. That year, war broke out again.

The Confederate battle flag had thirteen stars to represent the thirteen states that were supposed to leave the union.

A Flag for the Confederacy

For some time Northerners had been arguing with Southerners over the question of slavery. Northerners didn't think it was right that black people could be bought, sold, and treated unfairly by rich Southern landowners. Southerners said they needed the black slaves to help them raise their huge cotton and tobacco crops. In 1861, seven Southern states dropped out, or "seceded," from the Union. They called themselves the Confederacy and designed a new flag: the Stars and Bars.

At first, the Stars and Bars looked much like the Stars and Stripes. The field was three wide stripes, two red and one white. A circle of white stars sat in the blue canton. But Southerners decided it was too easy to confuse their flag with the American flag, so they changed the design. The new Stars and Bars had a large blue cross over a field of red. Along the arms of the cross were thirteen white stars. There were only eleven states in the Confederacy, but leaders kept hoping that at least two of the border states of Missouri, Maryland, or Kentucky would join.

Many Northerners thought the stars of the seceding southern states should be taken out of the American flag. But President Abraham Lincoln said no. He was determined to hold the Union together. Throughout the Civil War, the American flag kept all its stars. In fact, the number of stars grew to thirty-five after West Virginia became a state in 1863.

By 1900, ten more states had entered the Union. Each year that new states entered, a new flag was made. Since 1775, the United States has had twenty-eight different flags. All but the first one have had stars and stripes. Most of the changes in the flag happened in the nineteenth century when the nation was growing quickly. During those hundred years, America went through twenty-one different flags!

BELLAMY'S PLEDGE TO AMERICA

In the Pledge of Allegiance, Americans "pledge," or promise, their "allegiance," or loyalty, to the flag. By being loyal to the flag, they are being loyal to their country. The Pledge of Allegiance is not as old as the flag itself. It was written in 1892 by Francis Bellamy. He worked for a children's magazine called *The Youth's Companion*. Bellamy had worked hard to make October 12 a national holiday, Columbus Day.

> "I pledge allegiance to the flag of the United States of America and to the Republic, for which it stands, one Nation under God, indivisible, with liberty and justice for all."

The first celebration was in 1892. Children in cities and towns across the country celebrated with flags and special programs. The editor of *The Youth's Companion*, James Upham, wanted a special salute to honor the flag. He asked Francis Bellamy to write it. The "Pledge of Allegiance" was said for the first time on Columbus Day in 1892. Children in more than 120,000 schools across the country joined in the very first salute to the flag.

C H A P T E R

3

THE TURN OF THE CENTURY AND WORLD WAR I

War came again as America neared the turn of the century. Ninety miles south of Florida, American soldiers were fighting on the island of Cuba. The United States wanted to free Cuba from Spanish rule. Leading the American troops known as the Rough Riders was future president Theodore Roosevelt. The most important spot for the Rough Riders to capture on the island was San Juan Hill. Spanish forts atop the hill guarded the Cuban city of Santiago. In July 1898, Roosevelt's troops charged up San Juan Hill and captured the Spanish forts. A famous photograph shows Teddy Roosevelt and his Rough Riders at the top of the hill. In the center of the picture, behind the men, stands the American flag.

Opposite:
In 1898, Teddy Roosevelt raised the American flag in Cuba, after he led his troops in a successful charge at San Juan Hill.

The forty-five-star flag was in use at the turn of the century.

When the soldiers returned home to victory parades, marching bands across the country had a special tune ready to play. The new music was written by a famous composer and band leader, John Philip Sousa. The March King, as Sousa was called, wrote more than a hundred marches in his lifetime, many of them about patriotic ideas. The one written in 1897 became his most famous: "The Stars and Stripes Forever."

The flag made musical history of another kind in 1906. George M. Cohan, who called himself the "Yankee Doodle Boy," wrote a song called "You're a Grand Old Flag," which became a quick hit around the nation. "You're a grand old flag, you're a high-flying flag, and forever in peace may you wave . . ." the song begins. Through the years Cohan wrote many more patriotic songs, including "Over There," which became a favorite of America's armed forces during World War I.

America entered World War I in 1917, flying a forty-eight-star flag. During the first twelve years of the twentieth century, the country had added three more states: Oklahoma, New Mexico, and Arizona. The canton now had six rows of stars with eight stars in each row. Soon the forty-eight-star flag began to appear on colorful posters across the country, urging Americans to "Join the Army," "Answer the Call to Duty...For Home and Country." The flag was also used to help the war effort by stirring patriotism in Americans who were not in the military.

American soldiers answered the call, carrying the Stars and Stripes with them to Europe. When they returned home in 1918 at the end of World War I, their flag had not changed. In fact, for forty-seven years—from 1912 to 1959—Old Glory looked the same. The forty-eight-star design was the longest-lived of any American flag.

The Beginning of a Flag Code

Once the flag's canton stopped changing, government leaders decided it was time to make a set of rules giving sizes and measurements for our national banner. President William Howard Taft gave the first orders about design of the flag on June 24, 1912. Eleven years later, on Flag Day, leaders from sixty-eight patriotic groups met in the nation's capital. They drew up a set of rules outlining proper and respectful handling of the flag. In 1942, Congress put all these ideas into a code that became a law. The Flag Code is a list of rules about the flag. It gives sizes for all parts of the flag, from the stripes to the canton. It also tells about how to carry, handle, display, and treat the flag respectfully.

According to the code, the flag should be nearly twice as wide as it is deep. The canton must run down to the top of the eighth stripe. The Flag Code gives sizes and colors for the stars and the stripes. It says flags flown indoors, such as in courtrooms, may be decorated with gold cord and tassels.

HOW TO TREAT THE FLAG

If you are in charge of raising, lowering, or carrying the flag for your school, scout troop, or other group, you must follow the Flag Code. You need to know the rules about displaying the flag, folding it, and carrying it. Here are just a few of those rules.

★ The flag should be raised swiftly and lowered ceremoniously.

★ The flag should be displayed near the front of every school and government building.

★ The flag should be flown any day the weather is good, especially on government holidays.

★ The flag should not be put out in bad weather unless it is an all-weather flag.

★ The flag may be flown at night only if it is properly lighted.

★ The flag should never touch the ground.

★ The flag should never have anything added or attached to it.

★ In the United States, no other flag may be flown higher than the American flag except at United Nations headquarters.

★ On Memorial Day, the flag should be flown at half-mast only until noon.

★ At the unveiling of a statue or monument, the flag should be a special feature but never a cover.

★ The flag should never be dipped, or bow for any reason.

★ When the American flag is carried in a parade or placed in a group with other flags, it must be to the right of them.

★ When displayed in a circle, the American flag must be in the center.

★ A worn-out flag, when it is "no longer a fitting emblem for display" should be destroyed in a dignified way, preferably by burning.

Special Uses for the Flag

Most of the time, the flag is flown at the top of the flagpole. But the flag can sometimes be flown in other ways. These other ways are used only for very specific reasons. And they are only used once in a while.

When a government leader or important person dies, the flag is often flown at "half-mast," halfway up the flagpole. Flying it at half-mast shows that a city, state, or country is mourning over a person's death. When the flag is flown at half-mast, it is raised to the top of the pole first, then it is lowered to the halfway position. At night, the half-mast flag is raised to the top of the pole before being lowered.

According to the Flag Code, there is only one time when the flag may be flown upside down. That is in time of very great danger, such as during a war or when a ship is sinking. The upside-down flag is a signal of distress. In the past, some people have flown the flag upside down as a way of protesting against the government.

When a person in the military dies, a flag sometimes covers the casket. When the flag is used in this way, the canton is laid over the head end of the casket, where the person's left shoulder would be. Before the casket is put in the ground, the flag is folded into a triangular bundle with the stars showing. The bundle is then given to the person's family. The Flag Code explains just how to fold the flag in addition to explaining all the other special uses for the Stars and Stripes.

HOW TO FOLD THE FLAG

1. One person holds each end. Flag must not touch the ground.

2. Flag is folded in half length-wise, two times.

3. From the fly end the corner is folded over to the opposite edge to form a triangle.

4. With flag held taut, triangle is folded over on itself. This forms another triangle.

5. Repeated triangles are formed until entire flag is folded.

33

C H A P T E R

4

WORLD WAR II AND THE 1950s

During the 1940s and 1950s, *Life* magazine was a favorite of millions of Americans. The image on the cover of *Life*'s July 4, 1942, issue featured a large American flag. This was the country's first Independence Day after the United States entered World War II. Magazine editors must have known that Americans wanted to rally behind their country. The American flag appeared on more than three hundred other Independence Day covers that year!

As it had during World War I, the flag became the theme of thousands of military posters, urging people to join the service. A tattered flag flying at half-mast amid clouds of black smoke and fire is the

Opposite:
The forty-eight-star flag was raised by American forces after they captured the island of Iwo Jima, south of Japan, during World War II.

picture on one famous World War II poster. Beneath the flag are the words "Remember Dec. 7th!" That was the day in 1941 that Japan bombed American ships in a surprise attack at Pearl Harbor, Hawaii. It was this event that brought the United States into the war. The U.S. Treasury tried to raise money for the war. It put up many posters asking people to buy war bonds. One poster showed a GI (a soldier), holding a huge American flag. Beneath the flag was the phrase, "To Have and to Hold," and with it, in big letters: WAR BONDS. The image of the flag was meant to stir feelings of pride in Americans. It was hoped that the flag would help to rally people in support of the war.

A SMALL ISLAND

One of the flag's proudest moments came during World War II on the Japanese island of Iwo Jima. After fierce fighting, Americans finally captured this important Pacific Island from Japan on February 23, 1945. Marines grabbed a piece of pipe, tied an American flag to it, and jammed it into the rocky peak of Mount Suribachi. *Life* magazine photographer Joe Rosenthal snapped a picture. Actually this was the second flag-raising on Iwo Jima that day. Troops had raised the flag earlier, the moment the island was captured. That time, one of their own marines took the picture. The *Life* photo of the Iwo Jima flag-raising became so famous that it was chosen as the model for the Marine Corps Memorial, a monument in Washington, D.C.

The Patriotic Postwar Years

At the end of World War II, several countries made an agreement to work together toward international peace. They formed an organization called the United Nations. Its job was to keep peace in the world. In front of the United Nations headquarters in New York City, the flag of each member country flies from a pole. Among these is the American flag. This is the only place in the United States where another flag may fly higher than the American flag. Above the flags of all its members stands the United Nations flag. It is light blue with a circle of olive branches in the center. The olive branches stand for peace.

The flag display at the United Nations in New York City features flags from countries all over the world.

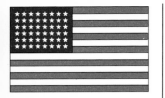

The forty-eight-star flag.

The 1950s were patriotic years for most Americans. Dwight D. Eisenhower, the general who had led American forces to victory in World War II, was president. It seemed that everywhere Eisenhower traveled there were parades, bands, and flags waving. Red, white, and blue bunting—a heavy cloth like that used for making flags—was draped from windows and on cars during parades.

The End of the Forty-eight-Star Flag

During most of Eisenhower's years as president, America flew the forty-eight-star flag. But on January 3, 1959, Alaska entered the Union. This new state caused the first change in the American flag in forty-seven years. Old Glory's canton now had seven rows of seven stars each.

Just eight months later, on August 21, Hawaii became a state. But because new stars are added to the flag only once a year, on July 4, Americans had to wait another whole year to fly a fifty-star flag.

State Flags

Every state has had its own flag for many years. But there was little interest in flying them until after World War II. Each state or territory has its own different flag. Some, like Puerto Rico, Mississippi, and Hawaii, use a Stars and Stripes or Stars and Bars design. Their designs remind us of the Confederate, British, or American flags.

Other states use a plain field with a picture, seal, or motto in the middle. Wyoming's flag has a buffalo. California's shows a bear with one star near its head and the phrase "California Republic" beneath it. The Colorado flag displays a large red *C* in the left half with a yellow sun within the curve. When a state flag flies alone, it may fly in the highest position. But when the American flag is present, the state flag must be slightly lower.

Other Patriotic Symbols

Along with the United Nations flag, our own American flag, and a flag for each of the states, there is a special flag for the president of the United States. The president's flag has a navy-blue field with a large circle of white stars. In the circle is the Great Seal of the United States with the bald eagle at its center. America's national bird holds in its mouth a banner that shows our nation's motto, *E Pluribus Unum*, "Out of many, one."

One of our most popular American symbols uses the flag as part of its design. In striped pants and a stovepipe hat with a star on the band, this character is often seen walking on stilts. He's America's favorite Uncle—Sam. The most famous picture of Uncle Sam appeared on a military poster during World War I. In the picture, painted by James Montgomery Flagg, Uncle Sam is pointing his finger and saying, "I Want You!" Over the years, that poster has been reprinted for many different uses.

THE FLAG
IN RECENT TIMES

During the 1960s, Americans began to question laws, rules, and regulations. Many young people, especially college students, were ready for a change from the patriotic ways of the 1950s. When they saw heroes like John F. Kennedy and Martin Luther King, Jr., murdered, some people began to angrily question their country's values.

For three days in November, 1963, millions of Americans watched President Kennedy's funeral on television. They saw his casket brought to the Capitol Rotunda in Washington with the American flag spread across it. They watched as a horse-drawn wagon carried the casket in a funeral parade through the streets of Washington—still covered by the Stars and Stripes.

Opposite:
A worker folds newly made flags in a flag factory. Flag sales skyrocketed in 1990 and 1991 because of the Persian Gulf War.

41

AMERICA'S LARGEST STAR-SPANGLED BANNER

On Flag Day, 1991, the world's largest flag was displayed in front of the Washington Monument in Washington, D.C. This flag was too big to be flown from a pole, so it had to be spread on the ground. It measured 411 feet across by 210 feet high and weighed 7 tons!

Making this giant Old Glory had been the idea of Len Silverfine and the Great American Flag Committee back in 1980. They took their idea to a flag-making company in Evansville, Indiana. The company agreed to donate equipment and time to make the flag. A textile company donated the cloth, a double-knit polyester like that used for grass-catcher bags on lawn mowers. In less than three months, workers had finished the Great American Flag.

But where do you put a seven-ton flag? The committee tried to get the city of New York to hang it from the Verrazano-Narrows Bridge. But there were too many problems. Finally it was given to the U.S. government, and turned over to the National Park Service for safekeeping. The Great American Flag was moved to Washington, D.C., on a truck with a forty-foot bed. Unrolled, this giant Old Glory is taller than a twenty-one-story building. Its stars alone are thirteen feet across!

The world's biggest flag.

The Rebellious 1960s

The very next year, many young people faced the threat of fighting in a war they did not support. American troops were being sent to Vietnam to keep communism from spreading into the southern part of that country. But many Americans could see no reasons for sending our troops to fight. They protested by burning military draft cards and marching in demonstrations. Some protested by desecrating the flag—treating it in a disrespectful manner to show their feelings toward the United States. This was their way of speaking out against the policies of the American government.

Flag desecration in the 1960s and 1970s raised many questions among lawmakers. The United States is a country of free speech. Americans can speak out when they feel the government is wrong. People who desecrated the flag said this was their way of speaking out against the government. Finally, a high court decided that laws about desecrating the flag went against an American's right to free speech.

An Act to Protect the Flag

In the 1980s, lawmakers decided it was time to think again about protecting the flag. In 1989, they passed the Flag Protection Act. This law made it illegal to "mutilate, deface, physically defile, burn, [lay] on the floor or ground, or trample upon any flag of the United States." A person could be fined up to one thousand dollars for mistreating the flag.

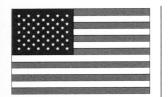

The flag we use today has nine rows of stars in its canton. Five rows have six stars and four rows have five stars.

The Question of Free Speech

On June 11, 1990, the U.S. Supreme Court voted five to four against the Flag Protection Act. The judges said that although it is "offensive" (not in good taste) to harm the flag, it *is* a form of free speech. "Punishing desecration of the flag," said one judge, "dilutes [makes weaker] the very freedom that makes this emblem [our flag] so revered [loved, respected]." With that decision, the Flag Protection Act was no longer a law.

Many people disagreed with the Supreme Court's decision. Soon there was talk of amending (changing) the Constitution to make flag desecration illegal. But Congress decided against this.

It is very hard to make changes or amendments to the Constitution. Since 1789, lawmakers have talked about more than ten thousand ideas for changes. Only sixteen of those ideas have actually become amendments.

Operation Desert Storm

During January and February 1991, America fought its shortest war, Operation Desert Storm in the Persian Gulf. A few people protested this war. But there was much more flag waving and patriotism than there had been during the Vietnam War. On nearly every street in America, flags were flying from poles and porches. Newspapers printed colored flags for people to cut out and paste into windows. It was a time when many people renewed their faith in the flag and the ideas for which it stands.

FAMOUS FLAG FIRSTS

★ The American flag's first around-the-world voyage was begun September 30, 1787, and completed August 10, 1790. A Boston ship, the *Columbia,* carried the Stars and Stripes.

★ Each time America adds a new star to the flag, the new flag flies for the first time on July 4 at Fort McHenry, where Francis Scott Key wrote "The Star Spangled Banner." President Harry Truman declared that beginning on July 2, 1948, the flag was to be flown day and night at Fort McHenry.

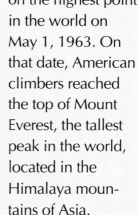

★ In 1909, the American explorer Robert E. Peary, along with Matthew Henson and four Eskimo guides, became the first to discover the North Pole. When the group reached the top of the world, the Stars and Stripes flew there for the first time.

★ Nineteen years later, at the bottom of the world, Old Glory again waved for the first time.

Admiral Richard E. Byrd arrived in Antarctica in 1928 and set up a base camp called Little America. When they raised the American flag there, it was the farthest south it had ever flown.

★ Old Glory was first planted on the highest point in the world on May 1, 1963. On that date, American climbers reached the top of Mount Everest, the tallest peak in the world, located in the Himalaya mountains of Asia.

★ The lowest ocean depth that the American flag has reached is 2,510 feet below sea level. On August 11, 1934, Charles Beebe and Otis Barton dove down, and with them went Old Glory.

★ One of our country's proudest moments was July 20, 1969, when American astronauts raised the first flag on the moon. Because there is no wind to blow a flag on the moon's surface, Old Glory had to be hung in a wire frame.

Chronology

1497   Englishman John Cabot explores America, carrying England's flag, the Cross of St. George.

1686   Colonists in the New England region create their own flag, with a canton of the Cross of St. George, and the rest a field of red.

December 16, 1773   The first flag of the United American Colonies flies at the Boston Tea Party.

December 3, 1775   The continental banner is first hoisted on the American navy's flagship the *Alfred* by John Paul Jones.

July, 4, 1776   American government leaders sign the Declaration of Independence from England, and a new flag is designed with stars and stripes.

June 14, 1777   Congress makes the Stars and Stripes America's official flag.

September 13, 1814   British ships attack Baltimore's Fort McHenry, inspiring Francis Scott Key to write "The Star-Spangled Banner."

1818   Congress passes The Flag Act, stating that the flag will always have thirteen stripes, and stars will be added for new states on July 4 only.

1861   Seven Southern states secede from the Union, calling themselves the Confederacy, with their own flag.

1892   Francis Bellamy writes the Pledge of Allegiance to the flag.

1916   President Woodrow Wilson proclaims June 14 Flag Day, although it is not an official holiday.

1942   Congress passes the Flag Code, listing all the rules for proper and respectful handling of the flag.

August 3, 1949   President Harry Truman signs an act of Congress making June 14 National Flag Day.

1989   Lawmakers pass the Flag Protection Act, making it illegal to mistreat the flag.

June 11, 1990   The Supreme Court overturns the Flag Protection Act, calling it unconstitutional.

For Further Reading

Bosco, Peter I. *The War of 1812*. Brookfield, Connecticut: The Millbrook Press, 1991.

Fradin, Dennis. *The Flag of the United States*. Chicago: Childrens Press, 1990.

Sandak, Cass. *Patriotic Holidays*. New York: Crestwood House, 1990.

Swanson, June. *I Pledge Allegiance*. Minneapolis, Minnesota: Lerner Books, 1991.

Voices from Our Country, A Sourcebook Series. Austin, Texas: Raintree-Steck-Vaughn Publishers, 1990.

White, D. *The Great Book of Flags*. Vero Beach, Florida: Rourke Publishing, 1991.

Index